.

Jason Irwin

STOCK MARKET GUIDE FOR BEGINNERS 2021/2022:

HOW TO APPROACH THE STOCK MARKET

Learn how the Stock Market works and find out how to get the most out of your investments

Table of Contents

INTRODUCTION

Is investing in the stock market really worthwhile? Is it as difficult as they say? How much money is needed to start?

Let's face it: the stock market is a dream for many aspiring investors who often think that it is complicated or that it takes a lot of capital to start and therefore give up.

Other aspiring investors actually start but for them the dream quickly turns into a nightmare with the loss, in whole or in part, of the capital initially invested.

I have therefore decided to prepare a complete guide, suitable for those who are just starting out, to invest in the stock market without making painful mistakes.

Let's start with the basics: what does it mean to invest in the stock market?

Investing in the stock market means obtaining financial profits by buying and selling listed shares.

The Stock Market is a regulated financial market where shares are listed.

Buying shares means buying a part of the capital of a company. Owning a share entitles you to collect a corresponding share of the company's dividends. In theory, whoever owns shares in a company has the right to contribute to the governance of the company itself, participating in the shareholders' meetings.

In practice, however, small shareholders have no power and their participation in shareholders' meetings is practically useless.

So, how do you make money in the stock market?

We have already seen that owning shares entitles you to receive dividends. Another source of gain is represented by the increase in value of the share itself: if you buy when the price is low and sell when it increases you can make a profit.

Few beginners know that it is also possible to earn when the price falls. In fact, the smartest investors are able to take advantage of any price movement in the stock market to make a profit.

How is this possible? It all depends on the platform you use to invest in the stock market: the best platforms allow you both to buy shares (to make a profit in case of a price increase) and to sell shares short.

Short selling is a speculative operation that allows you to make a profit when the price falls. There is no need to buy before selling short (this is why the term short is used).

In reality the Stock Market is not difficult and even those who do not really know anything can start without problems, provided, however, to study (at least a little), to commit themselves and devote time to practice in demo.

Unfortunately, many beginners make painful mistakes that result in losses on the invested capital or, in the best case, the renunciation of profit opportunities.

In this book I will discuss the most important topics a beginner needs to know in order to properly approach the Stock Market. In this way you will have all the tools to build your career as a successful trader.

CHAPTER 1 STOCK MARKET: THE BEST OPPORTUNITY MACHINE

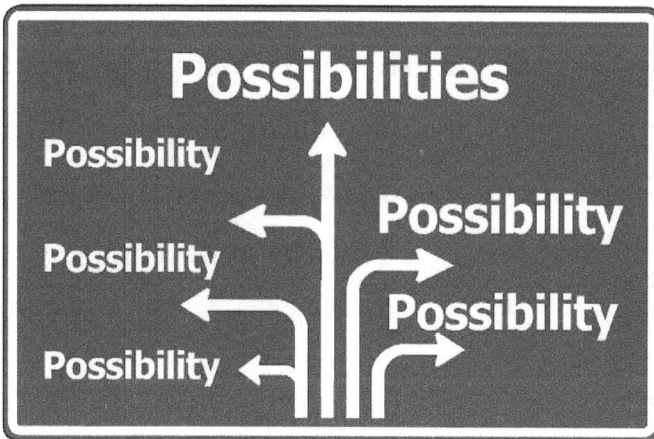

A stock is a form of security that suggests proportional ownership in a company. Stocks are acquired and sold predominantly on stock exchanges; however, there can be private arrangements as well. These exchanges/trades need to fit within government laws, which are expected to shield investors from misleading practices. Stocks can be obtained from a large number of online platforms.

Businesses issue (offer) stock to raise capital. The holder of stock (a shareholder) has now acquired a portion of the company and shares its profit and loss. Therefore, a shareholder is considered an owner of the company. Ownership is constrained by the number of shares an individual owns in regard to the number of shares the company is divided into. For illustration, if a company has 1,000 shares of stock, and one individual owns 100 shares, that individual would receive 10% of the company's capital and profits.

Financial experts don't own companies as such; instead, they sell shares offered by companies. Under the law, there are numerous types of companies, and some are viewed as independent because of how they have set up their businesses. Regardless of the type of company, ultimately, they must report costs, income, changes in structure, etc., or they can be sued. A business set up as an "independent," known as a sole proprietorship, suggests that the owner assumes all responsibilities and is liable for all financial aspects of the business. A business set up as a company of any sort means that the business is separate from its owners, and the owners aren't personally responsible for the financial aspects of the business.

This separation is of extreme importance; it limits the commitment of both the company and the shareholder/owner.

If the business comes up short, a judge may rule for the company to be liquidated—however, your very own assets will not come under threat. The court can't demand that you sell your shares, though the value of your shares will have fallen significantly.

What Is Trading?

Trading is the basic idea of exchanging one thing for another. In this regard, it is buying or selling, where compensation is paid by a buyer to a seller. Trade can happen inside an economy among sellers and buyers. Overall, trade allows countries to develop markets for the exchange of goods and services that, for the most part, wouldn't have been available otherwise. It is the reason why an American purchaser can choose between a Japanese, German, or American conduit. Due to overall trade, the market contains progressively significant competition, which makes it possible for buyers to get products and services at affordable costs.

In fiscal markets, trading implies the buying and selling of insurances; for instance, the purchase of stock on the New York Stock Exchange (NYSE).

Fundamentals of Stock/Securities Exchange

The exchange of stocks and securities happens on platforms like the New York Stock Exchange and NASDAQ. Stocks are recorded on a specific exchange, which links buyers and sellers, allowing them to trade those stocks. The trade is tracked in the market and allows buyers to get company stocks at fair prices. The value of these stocks moves—up or down—depending on many factors in the market. Investors are able to look at these factors and make a decision on whether or not they want to purchase these stocks.

A market record tracks the value of a stock, which either addresses the market with everything taken into account or specific fragments of the market. You're likely going to hear most about the S&P 500, the NASDAQ composite, and the Dow Jones Industrial Average in this regard.

Financial advisors use data to benchmark the value of their portfolios and, some of the time, to shed light on their stock exchanging decisions. You can also put your assets into an entire portfolio based on the data available in the market.

Stock Exchanging Information

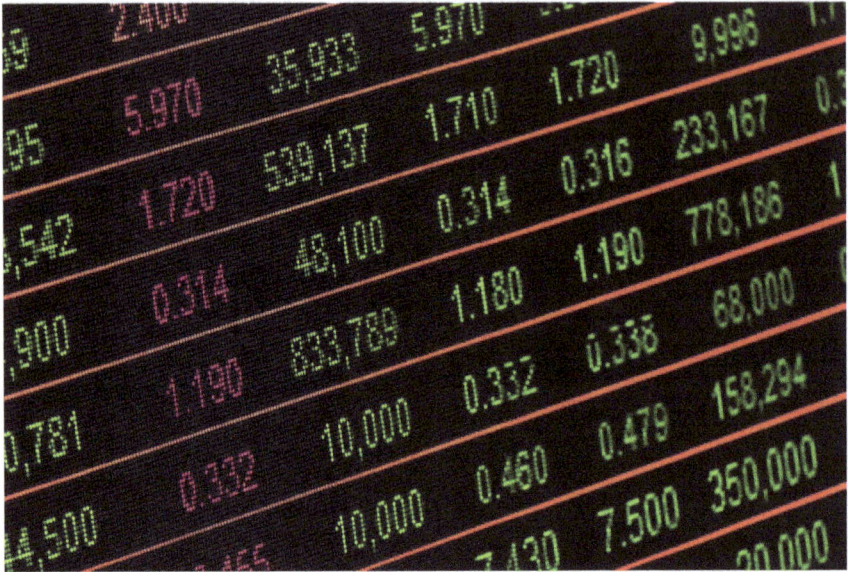

Most financial experts would be well-taught to build a portfolio with a variety of different financial assets. However, experts who prefer a greater degree of movement take more interest in the stock exchange. This type of investment incorporates the buying and selling of stocks.

The goal of people who trade in stock is to use market data and things happening in the market to either sell stocks for a profit or buy stocks at low prices to make a profit later. Some stock traders are occasional investors, which means they buy and sell every now and then. Others are serious investors, making as little as twelve exchanges for every month.

Financial experts who exchange stocks do wide research, as often as possible, devoting hours day by day tracking the market. They rely upon particular audits, using instruments to chart a stock's advancements attempting to find trading openings and examples. Various online mediators offer stock exchanging information, including expert reports, stock research, and charting tools.

What Is a Bear Market?

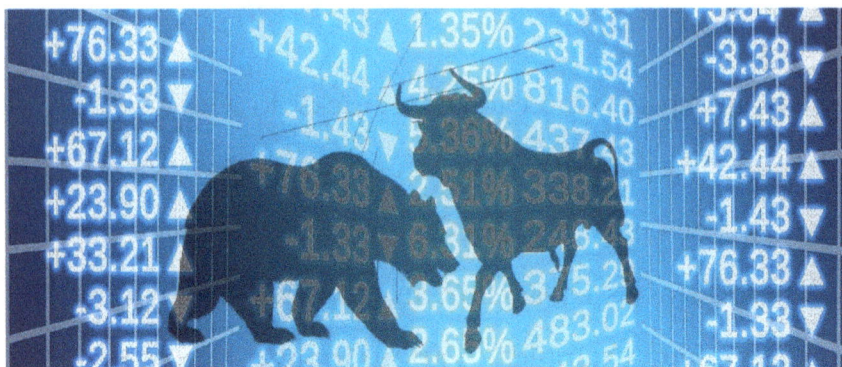

A bear market means stock prices are falling—limits move to 20% or more. Progressive financial experts may be all right with the term bear market. Profiting in the trade business will always far outlast the typical bear market, which is why in a bear market, smart investors will hold their shares until the market recovers. This has been perceived time and time again.

The S&P 500, which holds around 500 of the greatest stocks in the U.S., has consistently maintained an average of around 7% when you factor in reinvested profits and varied growth. That suggests that if you invested $1,000 30 years ago, you could have around $7,600 today.

Stock Market Crash vs. Correction

A crash happens when the commercial value prices fall by 10% or more. It is an unexpected, incredibly sharp fall in stock prices; for example, in October 1987, when stocks dove 23% in a single day.

The stock market tends to be affected longer by crashes in the market and can last from two to nine years.

The Criticalness of Improvement

You can't avoid the possibility of bear markets or the economy crashing, or even losing money while trading. What you can do, on the other hand, is limit the effects these types of markets will have on your investment by maintaining a diversified portfolio.

Diversification shields your portfolio from unavoidable market risks.

If you dump a large portion of your cash into one means of investment, you're betting on growth that can rapidly turn to loss by a large number of factors.

To cushion risks, financial specialists expand by pooling different types of stocks together, offsetting the inevitable possibility that one stock will crash and your entire portfolio will be affected or you lose everything.

You can put together individual stocks and assets in a single portfolio. One recommendation: dedicate 10% or less of your portfolio to a few stocks you believe in each time you decide to invest.

Ways to Invest

There are different ways for new investors to purchase stocks. If you need to pay very low fees, you will need to invest additional time making your trades. If you wish to beat the market, however, you'll pay higher charges by getting someone to trade on your behalf. If you don't have the time and interest, you may need to make do with lower results.

Most stock purchasers get anxious when the market is doing well. Incredibly, this makes them purchase stocks when they are the most volatile. Obviously, a business share that is not performing well triggers fear. That makes most investors sell when the costs are low.

The Comportment of the Stock Market

The stock market, like other businesses, has its ups and downs depending on the operations of how investors alter their financial prices concerning the market equilibrium.

Prices of stocks typically shift and may affect the stock market either positively or negatively. When talking about the market equilibrium, investors may become optimists, therefore driving prices to become quite high benefiting traders. Similarly, they may become pessimists, eventually driving prices too low, resulting in losses and a decline of stock value. This has led economists to debate and determine if stock markets are essential and useful.

According to the interpretation of different economists, there are multiple factors that contribute to these trends in the stock market. Some of the common elements have been linked to political and financial news originating from different sources. Irrationality in the market is another aspect but also depends significantly on economic news and other relevant market events. Crashes in the stock market are mostly a negative outcome when the stock market value deteriorates, leading to the loss of billions in companies and among investors.

Crashes are primarily attributed to panics, and loss of confidence with the most known crashes include the Wall Street Crash of 1929, Stock Market Crash of 2008, and Black Monday of 1987.

Over the years and the crashes witnessed before, different market analysts have come up with means of predicting how the stock market operates. Using trading strategies, the technique identifies online precursors based on Google trends searched data regarding shares. When the search volume is too high, it hence suggests that there are possibilities of losses in the future. Similarly, the decline in search volumes indicates that the stock market will become stable in the coming few months. The prices of stocks are usually captured in the form of stock market indices, therefore, vary depending on the search data volume. Some of the indexes include the FTSE, Euronext, and S&P.

CHAPTER 2 HOW TO START WITH STOCKS

Prepare Before You Start Investing

Many people who decide they want to get into the stock market are anxious to do so. However, it's important to prepare before you start buying shares. The first thing that every person should do is make sure that they have an emergency fund of cash stashed away, and that you will not use it to buy stocks or to cover losses. The purpose of an emergency fund is to have money on hand in case you hit the skids with a job or lose other sources of income if you have a car or medical emergency, or your basement floods and you need to pay for expensive home repairs. Recent surveys have shown that far too many Americans have been neglecting basic savings, and many could not even meet a $400 emergency car repair. If you are in a circumstance where you couldn't pay for a $400 car repair, then you are not ready to get into the stock market. You should work to save up a little bit of money first. Many experts recommend that you save up around six months of required funds to pay all your living expenses, and that is good advice, however that doesn't mean you have to wait that long to start investing.

Another important part of preparation is education. And congratulations, by reading this you've demonstrated that you are the kind of person who is willing to take time to learn before jumping into something! That is a very important consideration, especially when money is involved. You should also look into courses that are available online and read as many as possible, especially when trying to determine what kind of risks you are willing to take and how to marry your investment goals with that. There are many online courses available on basic stock investing, day trading, swing trading, options, and other topics.

In recent years the development of simulators is one of the most exciting tools for education. These can be useful, especially if you've never done self-directed investing before, but especially for those who are looking to be day traders, swing traders, or trade options. Practice makes perfect as they say, and that's as true with investing and trading as it is with anything else. If it's important for a football player to practice before a game, it's important for a new trader to practice day trading or options trading, before putting real money on the line.

Investing or Trading Based on Emotions Rather Than Facts

One problem with investing and trading is that emotions ride high. It's completely natural to experience emotional highs and lows as the stock market does its usual roller coaster ride. However, what you don't want to do is let emotions start guiding your decisions and taking you over.

The process of being guided by emotion can start at the very beginning when you choose your very first stock to invest in. Ask yourself a question—why are you choosing that particular company? Are you picking different companies because you think they are cool, or because you are taking a cold hard look at company fundamentals? You should be selecting companies based on whether or not they meet your investment goals. So you should be looking at their earnings, their future prospects, the P/E ratio, and other important metrics that will help you decide whether or not a company is in good shape both now and for the long term future as far as you can see it, and that the company helps you meet your investment goals.

Maybe you are in love with Apple. But being in love with Apple is not a good enough reason to buy stock in Apple. If Apple doesn't match up with your investment goals, you should be looking elsewhere.

Emotion has a huge influence when people are facing losses. People panic and sell-off. When the Dow Jones starts declining, people start moving their cash into "safe" investments, many that these days don't even pay hardly anything like money market funds. Most people don't even do that and just sell out and take the cash.

As an investor, you need to be disciplined. The courses of action described in the last paragraph that is governed by fear and panic are not the courses of action that a disciplined investor is going to take. Now if you are a swing trader and the market is declining, then either you're going to sell, or you're going to be shorting the stock. If you are a long-time investor, however, you most certainly shouldn't follow the lemmings over the cliff. What you should be doing is observing a downturn as a buying opportunity. So, you should be loading up on shares, but don't do it all at once. When the market enters a downturn, nobody can be sure how low it's going to go, so you want to make disciplined, periodic purchases the way you always do. Dollar-cost averaging always works when you are in it for the long haul. That doesn't mean you won't miss some opportunities, but over time the market will rebound again, and by the time you are in your retirement years, the prices will be much higher than they were when you originally invested in most cases.

There are going to be some cases when you're going to want to bail. An individual stock can decline for many reasons, and sometimes there is a point of no return. For example, Bear Sterns crashed from $170 a share to $2 a share over a matter of a few weeks. If you had invested in Bear Sterns, then you should have been studying the situation closely and you would have gotten out early.

So, you might want to bail from an individual stock when the data tells you that this is the right course of action. But you never get out of any stock simply based on panic. Know what the fundamentals are of the company.

Emotion works the other way too. When it seems like a stock simply goes up and up, people can start getting giddy about it. You might be tempted to put your entire life savings into that one stock. But that is a bad idea, no matter how good the stock is. It's great to know that Amazon increased so much that an investment of a few thousand would have made you a millionaire, but hindsight is 20/20. Right now, it's impossible to know which if any social media companies are going to actually bank profits and still be around in 20 years, so it would be foolish to put your life savings into one. The so-called investor who goes around claiming to know what the proceeding sure thing is can be called nothing more than a fool.

Another problem is people get emotionally invested in one company. Maybe it's because of the mission of the company or the products it makes that people think are going to "change the world." But when you get emotionally invested in a company, you start becoming irrational. Good examples include Tesla and Theranos. Let's take the latter case. Theranos claimed to have invented a revolutionary means to let people test their blood and to have medications delivered. It became clear that it was a sham, but the people who were emotionally invested in the company and the female CEO were fooled about it—and some still are even though it's clear now that Theranos is done and the CEO may even be facing charges.

In the case of Tesla, the jury is still out. They make high-quality products but have problems with delivery and scaling. They may yet overcome those problems. But if you talk to many Tesla investors, they are fans of it. If Tesla ends up going down the drain, many of the investors may go down with it.

To avoid letting emotion take over whether you get swept up with the lemmings running off the cliff when there is a bear market, whether you panic when an individual stock starts dropping, or whether you get hyper-excited when your favorite company is booming, you need to have rules in place beforehand and follow them.

For example, one rule that you could have in place is you never invest more than 5% of your portfolio in any single company. If you do that, then you are not going to be damaged even if you're a bit taken in by the company or you panic when it drops—or worse—miss when you should get out. Think about the poor fools who stayed invested in Bear Sterns until the end, and even the government wouldn't bail them out.

Long-Term Stock Investing

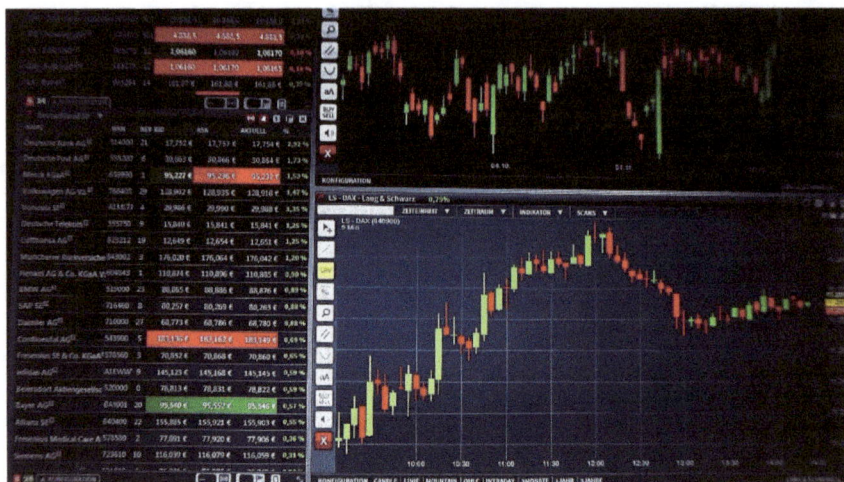

Investing in stocks is best viewed as a long-term strategy. If you want to make money for use much later in life, then stock market investing is considered one of the best strategies. This is because stocks, compared to all other forms of investing, tend to thrive with much better returns and resilience.

Stocks are indeed resilient that even those who purchased stocks in the midst of the Great Depression profited within a ten-year period. Also, if you take any ten-year period in history and examine the performance of investments, you will note that stocks outperformed all others including bank investments and bonds. This is true at least for the past fifty years.

Therefore, having the ability to determine which the most ideal long-term stocks are is extremely important. However, things do not end there because you still have to work out a lot of different factors. For instance, there is a large pool of stocks to choose from. You need to determine which are the most ideal and which ones are less ideal. Such decisions can mean the difference between a successful investment venture and a failed one. It could mean profits or losses. You therefore really need to eliminate all guesswork and ensure that you know how to choose winning stocks.

Different investors have different goals when it comes to investments. Some want to save for their children's education while others plan to buy homes or start businesses and so on. Fortunately, there is a large pool of stocks and industries to choose from. If you are wise you should add more long-term stocks to your portfolio to meet your investment goals.

CHAPTER 3 APPROACHES TO STOCK INVESTING

Setting Funds Aside

Investment means setting aside a certain amount of money and putting it to work so that it grows and multiplies over time. As the money grows, the investor continues with life as usual so that he or she remains productive. The money generated will then provide funds that can be used for any purpose at a future date.

As a prospective investor, you need to ask what type you are. This is because there are different kinds of investors. Brokers are keen to understand the kind of broker you are. This means they want to understand more about the kind of investments you intend to make, the amount of capital you have, as well as the frequency of trading you intend to undertake.

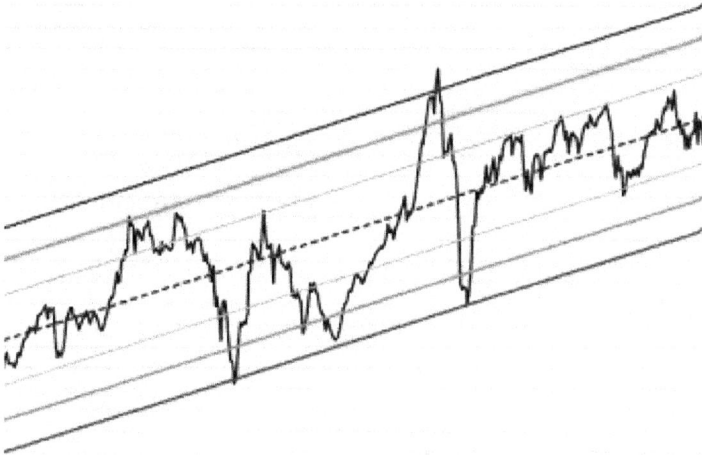

You will find that some investors are completely hands-on and prefer to trade on their own. Others are passive and prefer enlisting the services of their broker. The other types prefer investing via funds such as ETFs or Exchange-traded funds.

Online brokers are either discount or full service. The discount type has become so common that it is now the norm. Full-service brokers provide a wide range of services to their clients. They, for instance, provide advice about retirement, saving for business, wealth, and so on. They also provide additional services to high net-worth clients. They do charge significantly large amounts of fees for their services. This is normally calculated as a percentage of the invested amount.

Discount brokers are now more common because the majority of retail investors can afford their services. They provide their clients with essential tools that they need to carry out transactions on their own. They also provide robo-advisory services where investors get to set parameters then forget them and go about their businesses. Online brokers have provided their clients with additional services including mobile applications and effective educational materials.

Unfortunately, there are some brokers, including discount brokers, who have instituted minimum deposit requirements. As such, you may be limited in terms of brokers' choices depending on what you can afford. Fortunately, a majority of online brokers do not have such limitations and there are no minimum deposit requirements.

Robo Advisors

There are additional options that are available to investors. One of these is a virtual advisor known as the Robo advisor. There are some tech-savvy investors who came up with this creation. With the Robo advisor, interested investors get to receive appropriate advice about investment options and opportunities. It is said that over 58% of US investors use Robo advisor for investment advice. A Robo advisor can design a good algorithm that will help make decisions on your behalf. The algorithm will factor in things such as taxes due and so on. Also, data indicates that long-term investors fare much better with Robo advisors.

If you can identify some good shares in some crucial sectors, then you will improve your chances for success at the stock markets. Statistics indicate that diversified portfolios are much more successful and earn more money than single stock portfolios.

This approach will save you from imminent loss should anything negative happen. People have been known to lose their investments for lack of diversification. For instance, let us assume you purchase Boeing stocks, and shortly thereafter major incidents involving airplane crashes happen. The stock would plummet in value and you would lose most of your investments.

Investment Accounts

The main aim of an investment account is to generate profits and gradually build wealth over time. This is often achieved through the purchase of stocks and other financial assets over a period of time. Every investor looks to generate wealth for the long term. Investors often have different reasons for generating funds. Some wish to start businesses others want to invest in real estate and so on. One of the best ways of saving and generating funds in the long term is to reinvest interest and also compound the investments. Investors also diversify their portfolios into plenty of other products including stocks, bonds, options, mutual funds, indexes, and so on.

Investment accounts hold assets and funds for lengthy periods. It can take years and sometimes decades before profits are accessed. Investors take advantage of opportunities including stock splits, dividends, and interests that accrue over time. Of course, markets do fluctuate from time to time. However, investment accounts are able to override these challenges to grow exponentially over time. Moreover, the compounding of investments ensures that such challenges are overcome. Examples of investment accounts include IRA accounts and 401(K) accounts.

Invest Via Your Employer

Another approach that is common especially with employees is to invest via their employers. This is especially popular with investors with a tight budget. Therefore, if finances are a challenge, then you can invest at least one percent of your income in your employer's retirement plan. The benefit of using this approach is that you will benefit from having a growing investment yet you will probably not feel the pain of putting aside such small amounts.

Your contributions to the plan will be deducted from your pay each month so that by the time you receive your paycheck, the amount will have already been deducted. Now once you get comfortable with the one percent deduction, you can then think of increasing it probably to two percent or maybe even five. It is possible that you will also not miss this additional contribution. As a holder of a 401(K) account, you could already be an investor with funds diversified into ETFs and mutual funds.

Minimum Account Opening Amount

Almost all brokers will have a minimum amount requirement. This is the minimum amount of funds required if your account is to be approved. Therefore, before opening an account, shop around and enquire about the best deals out there. You may be surprised at what you are likely to find. There are brokerage firms that lower your fees if you maintain a balance of a certain amount. Others allow traders a number of free trades based on certain factors such as simply opening an account with them. Always consider such factors when opening an investment account.

Also, as an investor, you may not necessarily need a lump sum amount to invest in stocks. All that you will need is an amount as little as $100 plus fees and costs charged by your broker. However, it is advisable to grow your investments with time. This means investing small amounts like $100 each week, or every fortnight or even monthly. This is how a lot of people in America grow their money. They invest in the stock market and then grow their investments over time. The income generated is then used for other purposes such as capital to start a business or a down payment for a home.

Mutual Fund Fees

If you choose to invest through a mutual fund, then someone else will take charge of all investment decisions. They will invest your money on your behalf. Most people trust fund managers to invest on their behalf because of their superior knowledge and experience in all matters relating to investing. However, they do charge fees and these can be significant.

For instance, you first have to buy into a mutual fund. This means there are certain costs affiliated with just joining the fund. Apart from this initial joining cost, you also have additional costs associated with mutual funds. One of these is the MER or management expense ratio. This is an annual fee that ranges between 0.05% to 0.7% per year. It varies, however, depending on the fund type. Basically, when you buy into a mutual fund, you should ensure that you understand exactly what loads are charged. Loads are sales charges that mutual funds charge. They can be back-end, front-end, and sometimes even no-load charges.

Always ensure that you understand what these mean and what charges to expect. You should begin by checking your broker's complete list of funds and identify those with no-loads and those with zero transaction fees. In fact, these charges can be considered as a blessing because of DCA or dollar-cost averaging.

Finally, always keep in mind the importance of diversification. You have to diversify your investments to reduce and minimize risks. Remember that all investments are risky even though some more than others. To minimize your exposure, you should diversify your investments. This simply means that you should invest in a variety of assets even a variety of stocks in different industries.

There is a small challenge when it comes to diversification especially investing in the stock markets. Amounts such as $1000 or less are too little to allow for proper diversification. There are too many costs and charges that only larger amounts can cope with. This is where mutual funds come in handy. Since there are lots of investors joining hands, the costs are offset, and investing smaller amounts is possible and viable. Exchange-traded funds have plenty of stocks within them as well as other securities such as bonds so they are well diversified.

In conclusion, we have determined that it is possible to invest a relatively small amount of cash and enjoy a secure and diversified investment. This investment can grow gradually especially with regular additional funds as well as interest re-investment. You will also need to do your homework and conduct some due diligence to identify the most suitable investment vehicle for you.

Seek Professional Advice

One of the best ways of investing and harnessing the power of informed investments is to work with a portfolio manager or any other finance expert. Indeed, numerous investors invest independently without assistance from professionals. However, working with a professional makes it easier to diversify funds into different sectors and asset classes to monitor the performance of the investments over time.

Those who invest on their own will lack the kind of exposure, assistance, and wisdom that investment managers and financial advisors have. As an investor, you need to have proper information regarding all the tools and systems available to you. You also need to learn about any and all emerging opportunities as well as access to all resources available. This is advisable only for those who know what they are doing include finance experts, accountants, bankers, and so on.

On the other hand, while professional investment advice is crucial for ordinary investors, it does not come for free. There is a fee that has to be paid. Investors have to pay fees such as consultation fees to receive professional investment advice. However, the benefit obtained through professional consultations is invaluable. The professional has not just knowledge and experience but also intimate knowledge about finance and the various sectors. Also, financial advisors have legal responsibility or fiduciary duty to clients which means they are supposed to work in the best interests of their clients.

There are financial planners and then there are brokers. Brokers often purchase securities on behalf of clients. They act more like intermediaries between clients and the firms that deal in funds. On the other hand, we have investment advisers.

CHAPTER 4 HUGE MISTAKES THAT BEGINNERS MAKE

If you can avoid these mistakes when you are just getting started, you will be way ahead of the pack and will also save yourself a lot of losses and misery. Write down these "4 Commandments" on a sticky note and put it on your computer screen:

1. Don't buy stocks that are hitting 52-week lows.
2. Don't trade penny stocks.

3. Don't short stocks.

4. Don't trade on margin.

1. Don't Buy Stocks That Are Hitting 52-Week Lows

Despite what everyone will tell you, you are almost always much better off buying a stock that is hitting 52-week highs than one hitting 52-week lows.

Has a company that you own just reported some really bad news? If so, remember that there is never just one cockroach. Bad news comes in clusters. Many investors recently learned this the hard way with General Electric, which just kept reporting one bad thing after another, causing the stock to crash from 30 to 7. There is no such thing as a "safe stock." Even a blue-chip stock can go down a lot if it loses its competitive advantage or the company makes bad decisions.

A cascade of bad news can often cause a stock to trend down or gap down repeatedly. If you own a stock that does this, it is often better to get out and wait a few months (or years) to reenter. Again, there is never just one cockroach.

Never buy a stock after you have seen the first cockroach. When a stock goes down a lot, it can affect the company's fundamentals as well. Employee and management morale will deteriorate, the best employees may leave the company, and it may become more difficult for the company to raise money by selling shares or issuing debt.

Conversely, when a stock goes up a lot, it can improve the company's fundamentals. Employee and management morale will be high, everyone at the company will want to work harder, it will be easier to recruit new talent, and it will become easier for the company to raise money by issuing stock or debt.

If you stick to stocks that are trading above their 200-day moving averages, or that are hitting 52-week highs, you will do much better than trying to catch falling knives.

2. Don't Trade Penny Stocks

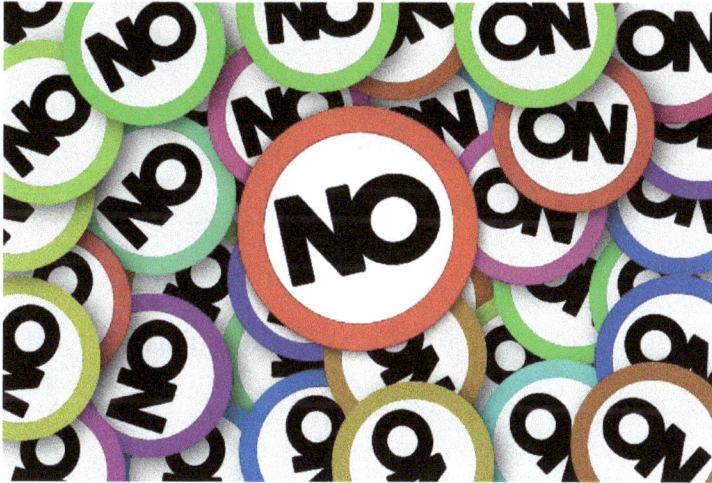

A penny stock is any stock that trades under $5. Unless you are an advanced trader, you should avoid all penny stocks. I would extend this by encouraging you to also avoid all stocks priced under $10.

Even if you have a small trading account ($5,000) or less, you are better off buying fewer shares of a higher-priced stock than a lot of shares of a penny stock.

That is because low-priced stocks are most often associated with lower-quality companies. As a result, they are not usually allowed to trade on the NYSE or the NASDAQ. Instead, they trade on the OTCBB ("over the counter bulletin board") or Pink Sheets, both of which have much less stringent financial reporting requirements than the major exchanges do.

Many of these companies have never made a profit. They may be frauds or shell companies that are designed solely to enrich management and other insiders. They may also include former "blue chips" that have fallen on hard times like Eastman Kodak or Lehman Brothers.

In addition, penny stocks are inherently more volatile than higher-priced stocks. Think of it this way: if a $100 stock moves $1 that is a 1% move. If a $5 stock moves $1 that is a 20% move. Many new traders underestimate the kind of emotional and financial damage that this kind of volatility can cause.

In my experience, penny stocks do not trend nearly as well as higher-priced stocks. They tend to be more mean-reverting (Mean reversion occurs when a stock moves up sharply from its average trading price, only to fall right back down again to its average trading price). Many of them are eventually headed to zero, but they are still not good short candidates. Most brokers will not let you short them. And even if you do find a broker who will let you short a penny stock; how would you like to wake up to see your penny stock trading at $10 when you just shorted it at $2 a few days before? I learned that lesson the hard way. It turned out that I was risking $8 to make $2, which is not a good way to make money over the long term.

To add injury to insult, a penny stock might appear to be liquid one day, and the next day, the liquidity dries up and you are confronted by a $2 bid/ask spread. Or the bid might completely disappear. Imagine owning a stock for which there are now no buyers.

Stay away from all stocks under $10. Also, stay away from trading newsletters that hawk penny stocks. The owners of these newsletters are often paid by the companies themselves to hype their stocks. Or they may take a position in a penny stock, send out an email telling everyone to buy it, and then sell their stock at a much higher price to these amateur buyers.

Watch the movie "The Wolf of Wall Street" if you'd like to see a famous example of the decadent lifestyle and fraud that often surround penny stocks. Viewer discretion is advised.

3. Don't Short Stocks

In order to short a stock, you must first borrow shares of the stock from your broker. You then sell those shares on the open market. If the stock falls in price, you will be able to buy back those shares at a lower price for a profit. If, however, the stock goes up a lot, you may be forced to buy back the shares at a much higher price, and end up losing more money than you ever had in your trading account, to begin with.

In November 2015, Joe Campbell broke 2 of the 5 commandments. He first decided to trade a penny stock called KaloBios Pharmaceuticals. To make things worse, he decided to short it.

When he went to bed that evening, his trading account was worth roughly $37,000. When he woke up the next morning, the stock had skyrocketed. As a result, not only had he lost all of the $37,000, but he now owed his broker an additional $106,000.

And there was no way out. If you owe your broker money, they can haul you into court and go after your house and savings.

If you do end up shorting a stock, remember that your broker will charge you a fee (usually expressed as an annual interest rate) to borrow the stock. In addition, if you are short a stock, you are responsible for paying any dividends on that stock (your broker will automatically take the money out of your account quarterly).

For all of these reasons, shorting stocks is an advanced and risky trading strategy. Don't try it until you've been trading for at least 5 years, and you have the financial stability to withstand a freakish upwards move in a stock.

And never short a penny stock. It's just not worth it.

4. Don't Trade on Margin

In order to short a stock, you will need to open up a margin account with your broker, as Joe Campbell did. You'll also need a margin account to trade stocks using margin.

When you buy a stock on margin, it means that you are borrowing money from your broker, to purchase more shares of stock than you would normally be able to buy with just the cash sitting in your brokerage account.

Let's say that I have $10,000 in my margin account. Most brokers in the U.S. will allow me to go on margin to purchase $20,000 worth of stock in that account. What this means is that they are lending me an additional $10,000 (usually at some outrageous annual interest rate like 11%, which is what E*Trade currently charges) to buy more shares of stock.

If I buy $10,000 worth of stock and the stock goes up 10%, I've just made $1,000. But if I can increase the amount of stock that I'm buying to $20,000 using a margin loan, I will have made $2,000 on the same 10% move. That will mean that my trading account has just gone up by 20% ($2,000/$10,000).

Of course, if the stock goes down 10% and I'm on full margin, I will have lost 20% of my account value. Trading on margin is thus a form of leverage: it amplifies the performance of your portfolio both on the upside and the downside.

When you buy a stock using margin, the stock and cash in your trading account are held as collateral for the margin loan. If the stock falls enough, you may be required to add more cash to your account immediately (this is called "getting a margin call"), or risk having the broker force you to immediately sell your stock to raise cash. Often this will lead to your selling the stock at the worst possible time.

When you open up a new brokerage account and you are given the choice of a "cash account" or a "margin account," it's OK to pick "margin account." A margin account has certain advantages, such as being able to use the proceeds from selling a stock to immediately buy another stock without having to wait a few days for the trade to settle. If you never exceed your cash buying power in a margin account, you will never be charged fees or interest. In that way, it's quite possible to have a margin account, but never to go on margin.

If, however, you don't trust yourself, open up a "cash account." That way, you will never be allowed to trade on margin.

CHAPTER 5 OTHER COMMON MISTAKES TO AVOID

Mistakes happen in every field, sector, and industry. Some are always anticipated, while others happened unexpectedly. When it comes to stock trading, there are several mistakes that you can make. Understanding these mistakes can help you avoid them, thus ending up successful in your stock investments. Here are some of the common mistakes made by most investors, beginners, and professional traders alike.

Failure to Understand the Trade

It is always wrong to invest in a trade or business you know nothing about. It is a great mistake to engage in stock trading when you do not understand the business and financial models involved. You can avoid this mistake by taking the time to research the stock market and stock trading before investing your money. Know the different markets, the driving forces, as well as trading procedures.

Most investors tend to buy stocks from the latest companies and industries they know very little about. Although such companies may look promising, it is difficult to determine whether they will continue to exist. Understanding a specific company gives you a better hand over another investor. You will be able to make accurate predictions about the company or industry, which may bring you more profit. You will quickly tell when the business is booming, stagnating, or closing way before other investors get this information.

Individuals who do not take time to study companies miss out on future trends of these companies. Failing to establish such trends leads to several missed opportunities. For instance, a person who invests in a company that is higher than his capital may quickly lose all his investment. That is why it is always advisable that you invest in the industry you understand better. For instance, if you are a surgeon, you can invest in stocks that deal with medicine or related stocks. Lawyers can invest in companies that generate income through litigation, and so on.

Impatience

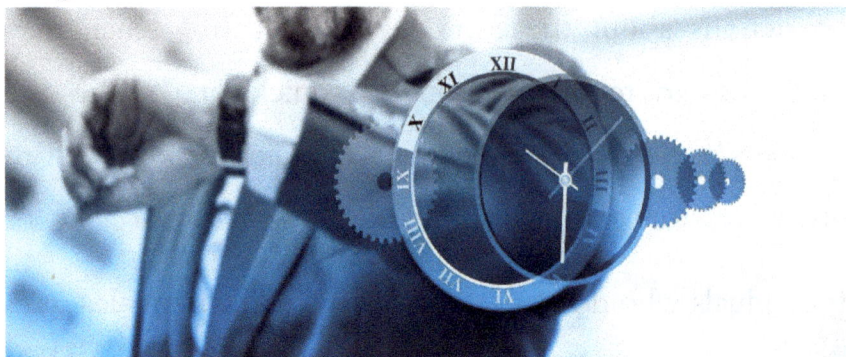

The stock market is for patient investors. It is a slow but steady form of investment. Although it bears various opportunities that can bring you money, you cannot make enough profit in one day. Most stock investors are always faced with the challenge of being patient. Some end up losing trade positions before they mature in the quest to make quick money. Exiting the market too early will always cost you some returns. As a new investor, you must never expect your investment portfolio to perform more than its capability, as this will always lead to a disaster. Remain realistic in terms of the time, duration, and resources needed to earn from the market.

Failure to Diversify

Another mistake that easily causes disaster is the failure to diversify. Professional investors do not have a problem with this since they can easily profit from a single type of stock. However, young investors must be able to diversify to secure their investment. Some of them do not stick to this principle. Most of these lose a great fortune as soon as they get onto the stock market. As you seek to invest, remember the rule of thumb governing stock diversity. This states that you should not invest more than 10% of your capital in one type of stock.

Getting Too Connected with a Certain Company

The essence of trading in stock is to make a profit. Sometimes, investors get too deep into a certain company that they forget that it is all about the shares and not the company itself. Being too attached to a company may cloud your judgment when it comes to stock trading since you may end up buying stocks from this company instead of getting the best deal on the market. As you learn more about companies, always remember that you are into the business to make money, besides creating relationships.

Investment Turnover

Investment turnover refers to the act of entering and exiting positions at will. This is one other mistake that destroys great investments. It is only beneficial to institutions that seek to benefit from low commission rates. Most stock trading positions charge transaction fees. The more frequent you buy and sell, the more you pay in terms of transaction fees. You, therefore, need to be careful when entering positions. Do not get in or exit too early. Have a rough idea of when you want to close positions so that you do not miss some of the long-term benefits of these positions.

Timing the Market

Market timing results in high investment turnover. It is not easy to successfully time the market. On average, only 94% of stock trading returns are acquired without the use of market timing. Most traders time the market as a way of attempting to recover their losses. They want to get even by making some profit to counter a loss. This is always known as a cognitive error in behavioral finance. Trying to get even on the stock market will always result in double losses.

Trading With Emotions

Allowing your emotions to rule is one of the things that kill your stock investment returns. Most people get into the market for fear of losses or thirst to make returns too fast. As a young trader, you must ensure that greed and fear do not overwhelm your decision-making. Stock prices may fluctuate a lot in the short term; however, this may not be the case in the long term, especially for large-cap stocks. This means that you may get lower profits in the short term, but these may increase in the long term. Understanding this will help you avoid closing trades when it is not the right time yet.

Setting Unrealistic Expectations

This always occurs when dealing with small-cap stocks such as penny stocks. Most investors buy such stocks with the expectation that the prices will change drastically. Sometimes this works, but it is not a guarantee. To make great fortunes, people invest a lot of capital in these stocks, and then the prices do not change much. If these investors are not prepared for such an eventuality, they may feel frustrated and may quit the business completely. However, this is something that you must be able to manage if you want to grow your investment. Do not expect more than what a certain type of stock can deliver.

Using Borrowed Money

This is probably one of the greatest mistakes that investors make. Some investors get carried away with the returns they are making. As a way of getting more profits, they borrow money and use it to enter more stock positions. This is a very dangerous move and can result in a lot of stress. Stock trading is like gambling. You are not always sure how much you take home at the end of each trade. It is therefore not advisable for you to invest borrowed money in it.

As you try to avoid these mistakes, you must also avoid getting information from the wrong sources. Some traders have lost a fortune because they relied on the wrong sources for stock information. It is important to isolate a small number of people and places where you will seek guidance from. Do not be a person that follows the crowd. Take time before investing in new stock opportunities. Carry out proper due diligence, especially with small-cap stocks since these involve a lot of risks. Remember, you must trade carefully and implement expert advice if you want to succeed in stock trading.

CONCLUSION

Investing in the stock market can be really very convenient especially if you use the right tools. In fact, shares are one of the most profitable investments, but it is necessary to learn how to earn both when they rise and when they fall. Investing in the stock market thinking of earning only when the value of the shares goes up will always lead you to lose money.

Learning to invest in the stock market is not at all difficult, in fact, everyone can succeed. It takes study, dedication and desire to do: all these elements are fundamental and go hand in hand. Studying alone, in fact, is not enough: it is always advisable to experiment immediately with all the concepts learned using a good demo platform.

The more practice you do, the better you will succeed when it is time to get down to business.

Now that you have completed reading this book you are ready to go deeper, and the best way to do that is to keep collecting information, the right information

From the same series you will find:

STOCK MARKET GUIDE FOR BEGINNERS 2021/2022: INVESTMENT OPPORTUNITIES *Learn how to invest in options and how to trade in the stock market using the best trading strategies that work*

STOCK MARKET GUIDE FOR BEGINNERS 2021/2022: STRATEGIES *The most complete guide to learn the best trading techniques & strategies to starting investing in the stock market*

STOCK MARKET GUIDE FOR BEGINNERS 2021/2022: TIPS&TRICKS *An easy and intuitive map that will help you move through the complicated world of Stock Market*

www.ingramcontent.com/pod-product-compliance
Lightning Source LLC
Chambersburg PA
CBHW050452190326
41458CB00005B/1245